AN OVERVIEW OF: THE NEW RULES OF WAR, BY SEAN MCFATE

(WITH SHORT NOTES)

COL C. P. RAMCHANDANI

Dedicated to all those fallen soldiers who never came home. The heroes that were left behind in some unmarked grave thousands of miles away and just forgotten. They deserved better than that.

Contents

Foreword

The New Rules of War, by Sean McFate, is a thought-provoking book that is truly relevant to the contemporary geo-strategic scenario. This succinct, snappy, and simple-to-read book is not only informative but also entertaining. There are also some occasions when the author is provocative and controversial.

The New Rules of War begins with a disturbing question: Why has the United States forgotten how to win wars? It is more than the United States; it is the West. The USA (and the other allied world powers) last achieved a decisive victory in 1945. Since then, every major battle has ended in a stalemate. The New Rules of War offers an answer to this question: the way warfare has advanced, we have not. The book then presents ten new "rules" for winning future battles. These rules are most likely to be ignored by the traditionalists, but that's the main reason we are losing.

Modern warfare is much more subtle and insidious. It doesn't fit into any of the common ideas from the first half of the 20th century.

McFate believes that although the conceptual tenets of modern warfare have altered, the Western powers have yet to adapt to them. They still respond to conflicts using old-fashioned, antiquated, and outdated methods.

In his view, even though we no longer often see a state-sponsored war or a classic military-on-military battle, nations are at war almost everywhere in a different mode than what we have seen up to WWII.

If the US and the West don't realise this and make changes in their thinking, planning and execution, their enemies will outsmart them. He argues that even though the paradigm of classical war has changed drastically, our culture, military-industrial complex, and leaders continue to view it as a conflict between one state's military and another.

He tries to convince, with examples, that modern combat does not involve this type of conflict. Victory in war is becoming increasingly difficult to achieve. Success comes to the clever, not the strong. The United States used to be clever and sophisticated with the world's most powerful military but suffers from acute strategic atrophy. Without a solid strategy, even the most powerful army cannot win.

His ideas are not new. The so-called "new" paradigm has been around for quite some time under different names.

The New Rules of War by Sean McFate begins with a suitable opening in its Foreword, in which Gen. Stan McChrystal poses a question: How do we develop strategically adaptable leaders in a society resistant to change?

This is followed by chapters in which McFate describes how things have changed over the past century and how Americans (and other Western powers) have failed to notice these changes.

He claims, "Except for us, no one fights "conventionally" anymore." This, of course, is directed towards Americans but is equally applicable to all. His points are laid out in ten new rules of war, each in a separate chapter.

Lt. Gen. B. S. Rathore (Retd.)

Former Director, Military Intelligence

Preface

The New Rules of War: Victory in the Age of Durable Disorder by Sean McFate is a noteworthy polemic that gives insight into the changing face of warfare. He analyses the past, present, and potential future conflicts and comes up with a model of how warfare has evolved. In his words, the destruction and misery that war brings are always the same. In this way, war is timeless.

His 10 rules form the prescription that would correct flaws in the existing policies and enable victory in the future. The West, led by the United States, focuses on technology, weaponry, and full-scale decisive battles as seen in the recent past. He contends they are unable to deal with future conflicts. Strategic thinking requires adaptation before it becomes too late. We should prepare for long-term disorders.

Where he goes somewhat off the reality is that the fact that there are rising insurgencies and dissent within states does not imply that full-scale state-on-state war is obsolete. In a direct power struggle, war between states may be unavoidable, and large armies with the latest technology will fight again.

At some point, McFate may have also misunderstood von Clausewitz. Von Clausewitz said that politics, including diplomacy, should be used in times of war. In his list of 10 rules, he talks about important problems that warring countries face, like fighting mercenaries, a failing international order, and the rise of insurgent groups in almost all democracies. At the end of each chapter, there are recommendations that many of the old guard may find difficult to consider.

McFate's rules help readers focus on what's important and offer bold and audacious ways to fix things. Thought-stimulating narration of warfare through the medieval ages and the rapid rise and fall of states' influence in modern day combat makes the book even more interesting. McFate's analysis is convincing, scary, and not partisan. It shows how PMSCs are changing the face of combat.

This book forms an essential manual for the younger generation of combatants for lessons on modern armed combat. It is also a must-read for the people who make decisions about wars today.

Col (Dr) C.P. Ramchandani

28 September 2022

Acknowledgements

Authoring a book becomes more rewarding when it is done for the purpose of giving it back to the organisation. For my military knowledge, I thank the Indian Armed Forces, where I learnt the basics of the Art of War.

I'd like to give a special thanks to my readers, who have been my biggest supporters and pushed me to keep writing my books about military history and get them into the hands of more young military officers who are taking promotional exams.

To my family.

And, of course, to Sean McCafe, the author of the book "The New Rules of War: Victory in the Age of Durable Disorder," on which this overview is based.

Prologue

Why, despite having far more resources than their adversaries, do Western nations continue to either stalemate or lose their wars? Because they are still stuck in the mode of the classic battles of WWII. They hesitate to think in terms of the new norms that have appeared.

In the future, most battles will be fought by covert means, in secret. Being able to lie and deny will be more crucial than having a lot of weaponry. There will be classic wars, but they will not be decisive. Large military and super technology systems will be made ineffective. Tactical nuclear weapons will be accepted in limited nuclear conflicts. The nuclear embargo will not remain forever simply because the UN has repeatedly proved ineffective. Classical war rules are no longer followed, and there is no one to ensure rule-based order.

To be future-ready, the conventional warrior's mind needs to grasp the facts. The Rules of War are effective because they embrace the nature of combat.

This book is covered in the form of summary of each rule given in a separate of McCafe's book, to bring out the gist of its main points. For more elaborate discussion as well as examples that have been quoted to support the authors viewpoint, the readers are recommended to read the book under review.

This is followed by the short notes that give out the various aspects that are touched upon while making the case for the new rules that are advocated.

However, the readers are recommended to draw their own conclusions when it comes to application of these ideas and comparison with the present modules. Also, it may be noted that the term conventional warfare here applies to the wars between standing armies of a country against the other using normal weapons and not the Nuclear, biological, chemical weapons, nor the realm of cyber wars.

CHAPTER ONE

THE TEN RULES OF WAR

"

The supreme art of war is to subdue the enemy without fighting

– Sun Tzu"

Blanco

Rule 1: Conventional War Is Dead

In this chapter, Sean McFate supplies a brief history of the state-on-state conflicts that developed after the Peace of Westphalia (1648), which were the forerunners to the Geneva Convention and other ways to handle war, which he says are no longer needed because the people who start wars don't follow them.

His main argument is against increased emphasis on financing and developing technologically superior military hardware.

Amassing such high-tech military hardware and infrastructure is useless for a confrontation that may not happen. Instead, the emphasis should be on augmenting resources that work, like the Special Operations Forces (SOF). However, these SOFs too need to be "restructured" to put more emphasis on working inside the political domains.

In his opinion, the country needs other, less violent tools for winning modern-day conflicts. He claims that nothing is more unconventional than conventional war in today's world.

Rule 2: Emphasis on Superior Technology Will Not Save Us

This chapter's focus is on not investing in costly war equipment like the prohibitively expensive F35.

In future conflicts, the weapons of choice will be "low tech". The focus will be on weapons that are easy to get and hard to beat.

The "Third Offset Strategy," which seeks to develop robotics and artificial intelligence as practical solutions to future warfare, is useless against futuristic threats. Such strategies involve pumping billions of dollars into the high-tech defence sector and will never be used as the days of large standing armies fighting each other are over, keeping future trends in mind.

In his opinion, intelligent enemies will always be capable of outwitting sophisticated weapons. We need to invest more in such people.

"War is armed politics and trying to solve a political issue on a technical level is foolish."

"This does not propose we discard sophisticated equipment, but we should stop worshipping it," he says in his conclusion.

Rule 3: Conflict and Peace Never Exist; They Always Coexist

Many opponents of the USA, especially China, take advantage of the fact that traditionalists see peace and war as opposites, while traditionally they have always coexisted. Therefore, even if there is no "state-ojavascript:void('h2')n-state" or "military-on-military" conflict, there will always be a need to find and fight the less obvious conflicts.

He utilises the term "lawfare" as a form of combat against the international rules-based order.

There are many examples of how China is "playing" the US by using the media and controlling the narrative. Unlike conventional warfare, this kind of war does not conform to the classic concepts of war.

In his opinion, the US doesn't yet have a clear strategy for how to counter and use this kind of covert power that one country uses to get an advantage over another.

Rule 4: Hearts and Minds Do Not Matter

McFate is against conventional counterinsurgency (COIN) doctrine, which focuses on building a nation, winning back hearts and minds, and getting "legitimacy."

It has allegedly let the US down at every point. In his opinion, while this may not align well with our sense of justice, morality, or fairness, he gives other examples to support his position.

Insurgencies are like armed social movements, and people cannot be bribed; they will take your possessions but not your beliefs. History is replete with examples that, in the end, COIN becomes ruthless—the complete antithesis of its warm and fluffy interpretation that seems to exist.

Thus, he envisions a "foreign legion" stationed in "zones of chaos" to combat "incompetent proxy militias, smart contractors, and American losses."

Rule 5: The Best Weapons Are Those That Do Not Fire Shots

In this chapter, McFate makes the case that persuasion works better than force and that traditional military deterrence no longer works. Therefore, it is important to weaponize "influence."

It involves keeping an eye on and knowing your target; exposing false information, alternate facts, and trolls, among other tactics; and launching a counterattack with your messages to the target culture. The tone of your messages is more significant than the accuracy or truthfulness of information.

He also urges "velvet regime change," in which we aim to weaken and pervert excessively rigid moral standards against the population in the target countries. He says, "Who cares about the sword when you can control the hand that wields it?"

Rule 6: The Mercenaries Will Come Back

This fascinating chapter focuses on the growing role of mercenaries in international influence and warfare. McCafe highlights the lengthy history of mercenaries working for the highest bidder in conflict.

"You are a mercenary if you are a civilian with a gun who is being paid to do combat tasks in a foreign area of conflict."

Covering the fascinating background of mercenaries and calling them "the second oldest profession," he addresses common criticisms against them.

In an unlikely comparison, he says that people consider troops as their own spouses, while mercenaries are viewed as prostitutes. In his opinion, mercenaries and soldiers are the two sides of the same coin. He tries to break the myth about the common public's opinion and gives examples in which, while doing the same task, mercenaries are seen as butchers, while soldiers make innocent mistakes.

He stresses that the use of mercenaries makes sense from many perspectives. The US has recently openly engaged private military organisations to carry out its job abroad. "Future American battles may be outsourced," he speculates provocatively, as "renting out a force is less expensive than owning it."

Mercenaries facilitate any party with sufficient financial resources to use force and coercive deterrence. Mercenaries who fight for money are not the same as regular soldiers. They do not take part in traditional wars and work only in the "shadow war zone."

Rule 7: Different Kinds of Global Powers Will Rule

In this chapter, McFate talks about how the traditional nation-state is losing its power and how it is no longer the only group that can use military force.

The majority of the 194 states worldwide are weak and susceptible to internal uprisings supported both internally and externally. Therefore, while countries may still appear on maps, in reality, new kinds of authorities gradually take over.

Because nothing can stop it from growing, the recourse to private force will increase over the coming decades, potentially transforming the super-rich into superpowers. The ultra-rich can buy a new type of power in international affairs when anyone can hire mercenaries to fight a war.

As war becomes more commercialised, there will be an increase in demand for mercenaries. Organized crime, too, is getting wealthier and more powerful by using private armies.

An interesting discussion at the end of this chapter covers the concept of "deep states" and a distinction between conspiracies, which are led by individuals, and deep states, which are led by institutions. Citing an example, he says that the US military-industrial complex consists of three parts: Congress, the businesses that make weapons for the military, and the military itself. They have a tremendous influence over the country's policies on world matters.

Deep states wish to take control of the system, as is seen in autocracies like Russia, Turkey, Iran, China, and Egypt, where they have centralised immense power and authority.

Rule 8: Wars Will Erupt Even in the Absence of States

As in the case of Mexico, cartels are not just street gangs; they are regional superpowers. "Experts" don’t classify conflicts like these that are fought for material gain and wealth as "war," but this is where they are wrong.

Traditionalists cannot envision battles without governments. But most battles in Africa and most battles around the world fall into this category. This is how violence will develop in the future.

Traditional strategists who don’t understand how privatising war changes combat zones will lose soldiers in battle.

Hiring private forces makes it easier for people who can afford it to get into armed conflict. Private wars are now akin to a business opportunity, with strategies like any other standard business practice.

Rule 9: The Shadow Wars Will Prevail

Shadow wars use information as a weapon. Therefore, the use of "troll factories" and "bots" is on the rise, making it hard for reality to get through.

The media presents an opportunity for shadow fighters. The author cites Russia and Putin as examples of those who have mastered the shadow war. In this chapter, he explains in detail why Clausewitz, the guru of Western military philosophers, is out of date while Sun Tzu is exalted. His philosophy still holds that subversion will be crucial in future wars.

Plausible deniability is the shadow warrior’s favourite weapon. The author often paraphrases advice from Sun Tzu, "Outwit your adversaries instead of fighting them." This form of warfare stresses information dominance and acknowledges that the cunning mind is superior to the martial one. This is not how war is fought in the West or the United States.

Shadow wars will become the main form of conflict in the coming decades. They use ordinary people as targets and take advantage of how much a country cares about human rights. The West should think about this if it wants to do well in the global shadow war.

The West needs to learn how to fight in the shadows without losing its soul, or it will continue to get sucker punched by autocracies.

He concludes that "power no longer comes from the barrel of a gun, but rather from the shadows."

Rule 10: Success Can Be Undone

McFate views war as "armed politics," which means that success is as much a political achievement as a military one.

He emphasises, "There are easier ways to win than open conflict, and such techniques do not require a large military force or even a military at all. He quotes Henry Kissinger as saying, "The guerrilla wins if he does not lose." On the other hand, if it fails, the traditional army loses.

Using what we've learned from past mistakes over the past 70 years, a militarily weaker enemy could beat a militarily stronger one if certain conditions are met first. The US focuses more on tactical triumph than strategic victory, which is a reason big military powers lost in Vietnam, Iran-Iraq, and Afghanistan: because they did not convert their military triumphs into political ones.

Tactical warfare is hard, and military commanders are trained to win by using predictable answers that are good for complex problems but not enough for the complexity of good strategy.

Achieving strategic victory calls for a special kind of thinking. According to systems theory, intricate systems are amenable to a solution, while complex ones are not.

An agile strategic mind is more important than smart bombs, innovative technology, and having a lot of people on your side. Without a sound strategy, none of these tactics can win battles.

Conclusive Chapter

In this chapter, McFate goes over what he has already said about the need for more strategic thinking and a fresh look at how war has changed and how our enemies are now fighting it. He claims that "conflict has progressed beyond lethality."

Highlights of the main ideas in McFate's book are given below:

The answers lie in reimagining battle and altering our thinking.

Conventional war has gone the way of the pay phone, and studies show that most people who die in modern wars are civilians. Warfare is constantly evolving, and we must adapt or perish. Anonymity is the preferred weapon in the information era.

Shadow war is a choice for anyone who wants to fight without any consequences.

Future conflicts won't start and end; instead, they'll smoulder and go into hibernation. They occasionally detonate.

Since intelligence is more important than strength and technology no longer decides who wins a battle, we need to put more money into people than expensive weapons and technology.

Because the disorder is the normal state of things in the world, trying to change it is a pointless and never-ending task. The West must create its form of shadow warfare since combat is moving underground.

Victories will be lost not on the actual battlefield but the information front. 11.Today, people don't die for their country; they die for their religion, ethnicity, clan, money, or even war.

Military organisations are known to resist change.

Since warfare develops before combatants do, many generals have fixed ideas about how it should be fought and won. They need to be flexible and evolve better methods keeping in view the changes in world order.

CHAPTER TWO

BRIEF NOTES

Why is it important to adopt the unconventional warfare doctrine?

Since 1945, Western nations, primarily the US military, have suffered only defeat. Even though the Americans had the best troops, technology, and resources, they were unable to achieve any important goals and had to retreat after a long fight in Korea, Vietnam, Afghanistan, Iraq, and other places.

In the same way, militias with few resources and simple weapons have beaten major military powers like France in Algeria and Indochina; the United Kingdom in Palestine and Cyprus; the Soviet Union in Afghanistan; Israel in Lebanon; and the United States in Vietnam, Iraq, Somalia, and Afghanistan.

As a result, it's clear that the problem isn't related to larger troops or better equipment. It's all about rewriting the rules of battle. To deal with them, you might have to think about fighting future battles in unusual ways that don't involve huge armies and high-tech weapons.

What is Durable Disorder?

All around the world, almost 175 countries are involved in some type of armed conflict, which does not appear to be ending anytime soon.

These are all low-level wars that can endure for years, if not decades! Wars no longer end unless one side is destroyed. Modern fights can last indefinitely, with no clear winner or loser.

High-stakes negotiations, superpower intervention, diplomatic efforts, nation-building, or techniques such as winning people's hearts and minds do not appear to be successful. Many peace treaties fall apart within five years, and it seems like lawmakers have no power. UN directives and international laws also fail.

Conflicts no longer begin or end formally. Conflicts hibernate and smoulder because violence and peace may coexist. There are increased cases of "neither war nor peace" and "permanent wars" all over the world.

This is a durable disorder.

"Durable disorder" signifies that conflicts will not come and go but will continue in "eternal wars." The main thing that defines this long-lasting disorder is that it has a strange kind of armed conflict that keeps going on.

Elaborate Upon the Argument That the Conventional War Is Dead.

The term "conventional war" refers to conflicts between governments with significant standing armies where firepower is king and military victory is everything. Honour is vital, as are the laws of battle.

Today's combat zones are not the same. These are not traditional conflicts, but more armed interventions in governments with ideological disputes. Terrorism, cultural genocide, and other kinds of non-state violence have eclipsed traditional interstate wars. These battles are waged in a comparable manner as before the rules of the "Westphalian Order" of 1648, in which only states are supreme and everyone else is subject.

Later, agreements, such as the Hague and Geneva Conventions, were created along the same principles, addressing primarily interstate disputes. All other types of warfare were forbidden and regarded as illegal. However, these rules are slowly crumbling, as is the UN's ability to regulate the situation. Non-state actors are becoming increasingly strong. Nobody fights in the traditional way now. We are now going back to the unstable world order of the Middle Ages and the way it was before 1648.

What steps are suggested to make the military ready for modern warfare?

1. Future security force training should place a higher priority on special operations troops (SOF).
2. Psychological warfare and civil affairs, which can help organize people and set up proxy militias, are two examples of non-traditional skills that should be improved and used more.
3. Bold efforts towards radically realigning the military's force structure should be made, with support formations given full consideration. The top leadership should be recruited from among the special operations forces.
4. Priority should be given to information operations.
5. Investing in warrior-diplomats.
6. Bribes to persuade opponents to change their minds.
7. Other tools must also be developed. These include information dominance methods, strategic communications techniques and public diplomacy that address populations directly and, intelligent selection of forces that allow credible denial.

Why is having better technology insufficient to succeed in a war?

Superior technological machines, such as the F-35 fighter jet and massive aircraft carriers, are impressive, but they can never be used in low-scale conflict. Such high-tech weapons are ineffective against threats like ISIS. After World War II, there was no successful military operation that used high-tech weapons or large, permanent armies.

Future conflicts will be low-tech. Modern enemies use things like cars, drones, and bicycles as weapons to make explosive devices and use low-tech weapons that don't have electronic signatures.

The weapons of the future will also exploit information assets and diplomatic channels to further their cause. These conflicts are fought against an enemy who does not wear a uniform and is not a member of any standing force.

"Third Offset Strategy" and its relevance.

When it comes to R&D and funding for their conventional armed forces, this is the latest buzzword in the corridors of power in the United States.

In the 1950s, nuclear weapons were the First Offset; in the 1980s, precision-guided bombs were the Second Offset; and today, the Third Offset offers robots and artificial intelligence.

Through technological means alone, war cannot be won. Since World War II, high-tech forces have been routinely defeated by low-tech adversaries. Over-reliance on technology dumbs down the force.

The solution lies in investing in people rather than technology, as intelligent and motivated people will always be able to outwit intelligent weaponry. This is clear from what happened in Iraq and Afghanistan, where luddites stood up to the huge military and technological power of the West. Technology is no longer decisive in combat.

What is Lawfare?

Lawfare is the term that highlights the way warfare is fought by cunning adversaries by "Legalizing Warfare", that is, to make a war that doesn't look like a war or is a "Non-war War." It succeeds because its war disguised as peace.

The line between war and peace has become so blurred that all nations mired in the old rules of war are baffled. Washington has a buzz phrase for this: the "Grey Zone." Others have a strategy. In Russia, experts call it "New Generation Warfare," and it conquered eastern Ukraine and Crimea. Israel has the "Campaign Between the Wars." China's version is called the "Three Warfare' strategy". It involves using the space between war and peace for devastating effect.

Instead of winning on the battlefield, it wins by taking away the enemy's will to fight before the fighting even starts. It does this with psychological warfare, propaganda, and the law.

Controlling a conflict's narrative is critical to winning present and future wars.

In modern combat, grand strategy is essential.

What Characteristics Define a Sound Grand Strategy?

Strategy is not limited to battle and acknowledges that violence and peace can coexist. It is always changing and adapting, which means that resources must be constantly moved around to deal with new threats. It combines a country's all weapons of power, not simply the military ones.

It might be offensive or defensive in nature. For example, the United States' policy of "containment" was mostly about defence, while the Nazi idea of "Lebensraum" was mostly about offense.

The most crucial aspect of grand strategy is that it is long-lasting, spanning decades or centuries. A successful grand strategy outlasts political parties, individual leaders, and regimes. The United States used a grand strategy known as "containment" during the Cold War. Its goal was to hold communist expansion and roll it back wherever possible. It lasted for fifty years, from 1950 to 1990. Each administration interpreted it differently, but its core strategic ideas stayed the same.

The Grand Containment Strategy of the United States from 1950 to 1990

It consisted of four parts:

1. It aimed to boost US influence while reducing USSR influence abroad.
2. To avoid nuclear war, it evaded direct conflict with the Soviet Union.
3. It tried to avoid a regional "domino effect" in favour of the USSR.
4. It stopped the spread of communism by using several different tactics. Nuclear deterrence through mutually assured destruction ("MAD"), NATO efforts, coercive diplomacy, covert operations, proxy wars in places like Korea and Vietnam, "rollback" of communist governments through regime change, and aid to democratic nations were among them.

These parts of containment were kept by both Democratic and Republican governments, but they did so in slightly diverse ways.

How is the strategy of Winning Hearts flawed when it comes to counterinsurgency?

Future conflicts will not be traditional since they will be fought against insurgents rather than states. History is witness to the fact that only ruthless tenacity and strategic patience can destroy the roots of insurrection.

Technically, the idea of winning hearts and minds is wrong because it only prolongs the conflict. The failure of modern COIN in Iraq and Afghanistan is proof of this.

Because all people cannot be bribed. They are either ideologically driven or eager or unwilling sympathisers with the insurgency. Therefore, supplying improved social services or creating schools, roads, or hospitals would never succeed.

What successful COIN techniques does the author advocate?

No one won by winning hearts and minds. Here are three tried-and-true COIN tactics that can work.

1. **Drain the Swamp concept** - Guerrillas blend in with the local population to survive. Hence the biggest challenge is finding insurgents. This solution is to drain the swamp, exposing the fish so you can kill them. Most of the time, this means bombing the people until the insurgency is over, no matter how many other people get hurt.
2. **Export and Relocation Strategy** - Spread the protesters out so that they are a minority in someone else's country. This will stop the insurgency for good.
3. **Import and Dilute Strategy** – Potential insurgencies are stifled when the indigenous population is diluted with your own. For example, China brought in millions of Han Chinese, which made Tibetans a minority in their own country and made them easier to take over.

The most effective way to end uprisings is to use all three methods at the same time.

The Advantages of Deploying a Foreign Legion

The endurance of special operations soldiers is limited. If everything is set up right, a Foreign Legion that recruits enlisted people from outside the country can build a huge pool of people and be a solution where everyone benefits.

They can track down foes in the shadows, where they breed, before they grow into full-fledged insurgencies.

How are modern wars won in the absence of direct military action?

Political power no longer flows from the barrel of a gun. There is no need to threaten military action to destabilise any country. The importance of force is getting less and less important, and this trend will continue, making large forces useless in future wars.

Today, all elements of political authority must be employed. In combat, these alternative resources can be extremely effective. Astute strategists can weaponize practically anything, even refugee waves.

Influence is more powerful than guns in modern combat. Controlling the narrative and weaponizing influence helps in winning the modern wars.

Strategies for wielding power and setting up information superiority.

Monitoring: This entails finding who is communicating what to whom, as well as how and why. As Sun Tzu advises, "Understand your adversary."

Discrediting: Identifying and exposing fake news, bots, trolls, alternative facts, fake stories, viral memes, and negative frames. Myth-busting must occur, or people will begin to believe the disinformation.

Counterattacking: This needs the addition of more weapons to the influence armoury. Among these are:

- Denigration Negative propaganda to generate uncertainty.
- Involuntary internalisation: covertly sponsor suitably disguised popular TV shows in countries with repressive regimes.
- Resort to Velvet Regime Change with some covert help.
- Indulging in the moral corruption of the adversary's support base.

It is more powerful to shape people's perceptions of reality than to mobilise a carrier strike group. It has the potential to destabilise governments, damage national unity, and weaken resolve in wars.

Modern Warfare: The Role of Mercenaries

Contract warfare is a new kind of war that has come about because international law and the UN don't work.

Since 2015, mercenaries have been active in Yemen, Nigeria, Nigeria, Ukraine, Syria, and Iraq. Many of these for-profit fighters outperform local troops.

NGOs such as CARE, Save the Children, CARITAS, and World Vision are increasingly relying on the private sector to defend their people, property, and interests in crisis zones. Companies that work in dangerous areas are tired of relying on security services from the governments of those places, which are often corrupt or not particularly good. As a result, they are turning increasingly to private forces.

Mercenaries are increasingly being employed in warfare due to their many advantages, such as:

1. Outsourcing clandestine activities allows for credible denial.
2. Most of the military history has been privatised, and mercenaries predate war itself.
3. Renting a vehicle is less expensive than buying one. Paying for one's own military troops is prohibitively expensive.
4. Private military companies are doing increased things that people used to think should be done by the government, like recruiting foreign armies and fighting in battles.
5. Long-drawn wars and conflicts, like we see today, are easier to sustain.

Mercenaries are therefore here to stay and will change the face of combat.

What are the "Deep States"

When a country's institutions of power, such as the army, the judiciary, intelligence agencies, and so on, go rogue and, instead of serving the state, make the state serve them, they become a "state within a state" that affects policy without consideration for legitimate leadership or citizens' concerns.

In other words, these rogue institutions seize control of the country from deep within the state's own structure. When bad government policies stay the same no matter who is president or prime minister, it could be a sign of a "deep state" at work.

What Is the Distinction Between Conspiracies and Deep States?

Conspirators are typically people or groups seeking personal gain, such as in a coup d'état. Both conspiracies and deep states are bad for a country, but there are some significant differences between the two:

1. Deep states strive to hijack the system, while conspiracies aim to undermine it.
2. Deep governments function in the open, while conspiracies run in the shadows.
3. Conspiracies are made up of radical individuals, while deep states are made up of institutions.
4. Conspiracies have a fleeting time range, typically months or years. Deep states consider decades and centuries. They can change, stop, or undo legal government decisions without being held accountable or drawing a lot of attention.
5. When a deep state is endangered, it does not sleep peacefully. It launches an attack. It is one of the forces accelerating durable disorder.

What are the Shadow Wars?

Shadow wars are secret armed confrontations that revolve around plausible deniability. In the digital age, plausible denial of guilt is more important than having weapons, because no one can get the entire world ready to fight a war that might not even be happening. Cloaking is a type of power in a shadow battle, and knowledge is weaponized.

It's difficult to tell the difference between fact and fiction without convincing evidence. Warriors, like special operations teams, mercenaries, terrorists, proxy militias, little green men, and foreign legions, wear masks and have good reasons to say they are not who they are accused of being.

Shadow warfare is effective because it weaponizes information in the information age by distorting the enemy's view of reality. This is done by controlling the electronic media and spreading false information with the help of armies of trolls.

The Doctrine of Sun Tzu and Modern Warfare

Deception is inherent in warfare. "All combat is founded on deception," Sun Tzu stated 2,500 years ago. Sun Tzu says that you should take an "indirect approach" to war. Instead of fighting your enemies, he says, you should outsmart them. Sun Tzu thinks that using force is a fool's way to fight and that success on the battlefield is a sign of a bad general.

Don't rush into a firefight with your opponents. Instead, entice them into a firefight and mop up the survivors. Deception is used to generate disorder, which is later exploited. When capable, pretend to be incapable; when active, pretend to be inactive. When you're close, appear far away; when you're far away, appear close. Fake a breakdown, then attack an unprepared opponent. Deception throws your adversary off guard and keeps him wondering.

These are the strategies employed in modern warfare.

The Doctrine of Sun Tzu vs. Clausewitz

1. According to Clausewitz, sheer force and combat triumph are everything; according to Sun Tzu, they are nothing.
2. Chaos and "the fog of war" are cursed by Clausewitz as impediments to victory; Sun Tzu uses chaos and weaponizes it for victory.
3. For Clausewitz, ruses are weak weapons; for Sun Tzu, they are the preferred weapon.
4. Sun Tzu regards spies as indispensable.
5. Sun Tzu is the father of "unconventional" war, while Clausewitz is the founder of "conventional" war.
6. Sun Tzu is the ninja, while Clausewitz is the legionnaire.
7. Sun Tzu is the fox, while Clausewitz is the lion.

How Are Shadow Wars Different from Insurgency

Shadow wars can be used to imitate or hijack insurgencies. It is therefore important to be able to tell the difference between a real insurgency and a "shadow war" because they need different responses.

The simplest way to tell the difference between an insurgency and a shadow war is to look at how the locals are treated. Even the most ferocious insurgents need people, hence they are generally safe.

In shadow warfare, civilians are more than just a source of collateral damage; they are also useful military targets. There are no rules of engagement; people are targets. The international community does little to help them because of deniability by the shadow warriors.

What Do You Mean When You Say, "Victory Is Fungible?"

War is no longer merely a military confrontation of wills. It's a form of armed politics. This is the sole true law of war. As a result, there are many ways to win in war—victory is fungible.

Strategy does not always involve a large military, or even one at all. A war does not require a lot of firepower to win.

War nowadays is as much about propaganda as it is about battlefield achievement. This is especially true when confronting democracies because their citizens can hire and fire. The United States won the tactical battle on the ground in the Vietnam War, while the North Vietnamese won the strategic battle on the American home front.

A clever person can use practically everything as a weapon: refugees, information, election cycles, money, and the law. Power is malleable in a fight, and the smart and clever are more likely to win than the strong. Denying victory conditions to the enemy is a better method of winning than direct confrontation.

Explain The Fabian Strategy and Its Application in Modern Warfare.

Fabius, a Roman general, used it against Hannibal's superior army during the Second Punic War (218–201 BCE).

A Fabian strategy is a method of conducting military operations in which time is weaponized in a significant manner. In this case, one side avoids big, pitched battles and instead goes for small, harassing attacks to make the other side less likely to fight, and wear them out.

The weak can beat the strong if they are fighting for survival and not because they want to, or if they are protecting their country from an attack from the outside, are united behind a cause, identity, or philosophy, and are willing to die.

The longer the battle goes on, the more expensive it becomes for the strong in terms of troops, money, and political will at home; it becomes too expensive for the strong to stay, and they will eventually quit on their own. It is possible to win the war yet lose the military. Major militaries lost in Vietnam, Iraq, and Afghanistan because they were not able to turn their military victories into political victories.

Explain Tactization of Strategy

There are three levels of war: tactical, operational, and strategic. Tactical warfare is the most basic level of warfare, and it is the domain of the soldier. Tactics involve manoeuvring small forces on the battlefield and carrying out airstrikes and specific actions at sea.

The operational level comes next. It entails merging many military campaigns into a single theatre of conflict. During World War II, in a theatre of war, in the European operations.

Strategy is at the top. Strategic war goes beyond military methods and includes all tools of national power—economic, diplomatic, social, political, informational, and military—that are used to further a country's national goals.

Failures at the tactical and operational levels can be rectified, but failures at the strategic level can result in the collapse of the entire house of war. Therefore, success can be achieved only on a strategic level, and the only legitimate measure of victory is this: did the war reach the goals it set out to achieve?

Tactical confrontations rarely change political situations on their own. Military leaders must train themselves to think strategically as cadets rather than colonels. By then, it is often too late. This is since tactics and strategy need two distinct modes of thought. One is easy, while the other is difficult. In the words of Sun Tzu, "Without tactics, strategy is the slowest path to victory. Tactics without strategy is the noise before defeat."

Books By This Author

The Korean War (1950-1953)

This book covers the gripping tale of The Korean War and is a valuable resource for students of military history keen to understand the power play in the geopolitical arena during the period that followed the Second World War.
The Korean War is about the guts and glory of those

soldiers who braved the severe winters, walked through minefields into the barrage of artillery, and sacrificed their lives, fighting from one battle to another for a long haul of three years, fighting a war they did not deserve.

At the end of the Korean conflict, both sides were almost exactly where they started, at an enormous cost in human life and property.

The book has been designed keeping in mind the requirements of the DSSC Examination for the armed forces officers in India.

Printed by Libri Plureos GmbH in Hamburg, Germany